Just Remember

Elevate and Celebrate Your Special Uniqueness

MARCY KRUCHTEN

We Will Always Love You
Marcella-Mom 1923-2011

Praise for Just Remember

I'm Olivia Kruchten, Marcy Kruchten's ten year old granddaughter. I have had many thoughts on the book that my Grandmother wrote. Ever since I read it it has changed my life. I hope that it changes your life too. She has opened my eyes to so much I had never thought about before.

Marcy, my mother-in-law, started this book after we spoke so many times about her life experiences. Her insight and humor give special meaning to advice. Marcy is someone who can make something wonderful and beautiful out of nothing. She can relay her joys and trials and retell her successes and what she learned from struggling in such a way that we all can relate. Anyone can walk away from this book with a little more understanding about how we all strive to achieve happiness in life. While also enjoying each day of the journey.

LISA KRUCHTEN

Barringer Publishing, Naples, Florida
www.barringerpublishing.com
Cover, graphics, layout design by Lisa Camp
Editing by Elizabeth Heath

ISBN: 9780983198932

Library of Congress Cataloging-in-Publication Data
Just Remember / Marcy Kruchten

Printed in U.S.A.

CALLA LILY PAINTING BY
MARCY KRUCHTEN

Calla lilies signify rebirth

Dedicated to

My Son Demian & My Two Muses
Olivia & Georgia

Acknowledgements

I am grateful and would like to thank these wonderful people for making this book possible:

Lisa, my daughter-in-law, for prompting me to write down those ideas for the girls.

Demian, my son, for reading the multiple drafts and giving me his frank and always interesting philosophical opinions.

Angie Hungrecker, my sister, for helping me to float above the madness with wine and laughter.

Jeff Schlesinger, my publisher, for having faith in my creativity as a writer.

Lisa Camp, my designer, the layout and cover turned out beautifully.

Elizabeth Heath, my editor, for her patience in getting it right.

Jean Smith, my dear friend, for listening to me ramble on and on over the years about my sometimes wild and crazy life.

Marcella Matanich, mom, for that sweet way you tilted your head when I talk about my ideas and my books.

Michael Matanich, dad, the true artist in the family, for telling me I was his doll. I miss you every day.

Marion Blomeier, my European mother, when I was having doubts, always told me to "just look in the mirror."

Arlene Helgeson, the mentor of my life, who set a shining path for me.

Finally, Pat Kruchten, for having faith that whatever quirky ideas I came up with, would somehow become beautiful. And for helping me to see the world, in a new way, through our travels together.

To numerous friends and family, who over the years have shared their lives with me:

Julie Wethington, Ginny Tennant, Inna Karachunskaya, Don Helgeson, MJ Cote, Jane Schultzentenburg, Sue Colt, Judy Jenkins, Pina Olson, Jeanne Geiser, Judy Scheuerell, Mary Margaret Kruchten, Sonia Kruchten, Sue Huff, Pam Foulkes, Jann Northway, Rosemary Kruchten, Lacey King, Chuck Stenger, Rose Edin.

Some are lost now, but what you taught me, I will always Just Remember.

~Marcy Kruchten

When you come to the edge of the light that you know,
and you are about to step off into the darkness of the unknown,
faith is knowing one of two things will happen,
there will be something to land on, or you will learn how to fly.

UNKNOWN

Preface

THE HOUSE IN ENGLAND

❧

As I was walking through a grand house in England several years ago, I stopped and as I stood there and studied that long ago deceased woman in the gilded frame, I realized that I knew more about what she looked like, dressed like and thought about, than I did about my own grandmothers. That is when I decided that I did not want it to be that way for my granddaughters. I would love to have known what my grandmothers thought about various topics, from recipes for apple pie to recipes for life. It was around that same time that my daughter-in-law said she appreciated my little tips on life and that I should write them down for her girls.

While on holiday, I woke up in the middle of the night, one night in Dubai, picked up some hotel stationaery and started writing. I wrote nonstop, for days.

So here are a few of the lessons I have learned.

Confucius once said that "we learn by three methods: First by reflection, which is noblest; second by imitation, which is the easiest; third by experience, which is the bitterest." I hope these little lessons on life I've compiled in Just Remember will help you to learn by imitation, by far the easiest way. So here goes.

The soul is nurtured by
want as much as by plenty.

THOMAS MOORE

Estate in England

CREATIVITY (A HISTORY)

Sometimes I wonder why I was so creative so early in my life. I think it was out of pure necessity and survival. I grew up lower middle class white. My father was a teacher; we had six kids in our family, so we didn't have much money. I was embarrassed by that and didn't want my friends to come over and see that we didn't have the ultimate at the time, wall to wall carpeting. Of course, I could see that there was a big wide world out there through movies and National Geographic. We didn't have television until I was a sophomore in high school.

When I had to draw a picture in the 3rd grade, I drew an African mask similar to one I had seen in National Geographic. Everyone marveled at it and after that I knew I had a special talent and I was thought to be an artist. I had to have a big imagination and needed to create beauty in my mind to make up for my stark surroundings.

When I was in the 5th grade I decorated our house in French Provincial style. At that point my dad had become the director of the school and our family was a little better off financially.

A friend of mine had a grandmother who owned a clothing store and unbeknownst to me, she became my first mentor. She taught me about clothing design, style, fit and color. That was the first time that I became aware of fashion.

I started to design clothing for my paper dolls and made paper houses from furniture that I cut out of catalogues. Because I could not afford much of the fashion I saw in catalogues, I started to design and sew my own clothing. I became quite good at this and was voted the best dressed in my high school class, which was quite a feat for a poor girl.

To this day, it still warms my heart to think about my dream designing. Little did I know that, years later, I would be featured in a magazine and called, "A True Original." Creativity is always a magnet to others, especially if you are brave and take chances. I have learned that neither dire circumstances nor lack of money can stop you from creating in your mind.

List of Contents

Chapter 1

BE YOUR OWN TRUE ORIGINAL

When you start to be your own original, you will be at first considered by others to be somewhat odd. Don't let that affect you. Eventually, you will be esteemed and honored for being original and will no longer be considered odd. People will start saying that you can do it or wear it, or carry it off or try new things. This is a sign that you are on your way to being a true original.

Always pay attention to everything and everyone around you. This will help you to open your mind to use colors, shapes and design for your future creations. Remember, true creativity is using old ideas and things in new ways. This is the opposite of insanity, which is doing the same thing over and over again and expecting different results. Even though others want to pigeon hole you, you will not let them do this. Your creativity will at first seem insane to them, don't ever let their uneasiness interfere with your creativity. Look around and use what you already have available. If you don't have a tablecloth to decorate your table with, use a dress or a cape or a pillow case. Press yourself to make do and you will be forced to use old things in new ways.

Start interesting collections, even if they are small and inexpensive. This helps you notice smaller details. Be bold and don't be afraid to be different. You are different and you love being different; what do you have to lose, only yourself?

After awhile, others will expect you to be different and you then will be on your way to becoming an icon. You can finally relax and trust your

15

instincts. Your creativity will finally be recognized for what it is, a true original, true power. Remember, the visual world is a universal language. In a powerful and admired world, create grandly and you will be treated grandly. Everyone has fantasies, your fantasies of flight will help others to see what you see and they will fly with you. Just Remember, be a dream weaver, not a dream catcher.

Dreams come true; without that possibility,
nature would not incite us to have them.

JOHN UPDIKE

Unmask Your Special Uniqueness
2011

Chapter 2

DEVELOP YOUR SIGNATURE STYLE

Develop your own signature dress style. What do you have to gain by blending in? Any type of style is OK, as long as you are true to yourself. Learn from the more adventurous and stylish around you. Ideas are everywhere. You do indeed have your own style. We say who we are, what we think of ourselves, where we want to go in life in a mere few seconds to everyone, if they care to be observant.

We are always judged by everyone around us. Everyone is always judging how old we are, our height, our weight, if we whiten our teeth, have had a recent facelift, to where we went to school, to our tax bracket. Aside from all of this, we are judged by the way we dress and present ourselves to the world, while we can sit back and do the same. Don't ever underestimate the joy a compliment or the happiness that attention can bring to your life and to others. Appreciate your youth, and enjoy it while you can. Enjoy every stage along the way and don't be so harsh on yourself; like my friend tells me, "Just look in the mirror." Just Remember, fashion is today, style is forever.

Be a first rate version of yourself,
not a second rate version of somebody else.

JUDY GARLAND

Chapter 3

PASSION IS YOUR KEY

ઢ

What moves you? What makes you happy? What makes you say, "I would do this even if they didn't pay me?" What makes you want to sing? What makes you try harder? What makes you take lessons to get better? What makes you want to take risks? What makes you want to be different? What makes you forget about the pain? What makes you go to the edge and even beyond the edge of safe to improve? What makes you want to get up each day and persevere to the next new challenge? What makes you admire the skills of others? What makes you not want to waste yours and others time? What make you fierce? What makes you do it all over again, after you have failed the first or second or third time? Just Remember, listen to your true passions, they are your true calling.

Choosing to act on what matters is the choice to live a passionate existence, which is anything but controlled and predictable.

PETER BLOCK

Chapter 4

STUDY YOURSELF

ॐ

Why is it that others can recognize our best qualities and when they tell us about these qualities we are surprised? Why is it that the thing that is easiest for us to do, is underestimate our special talents?

Don't be afraid to be unique and therefore special. Our uniqueness is what makes us different and makes us special, even if that quality or feature is odd, grotesque or even deformed. We can only be admired for our uniqueness, not our mundaneness and our sameness to others. Work on it, hone it, and own it. Enjoy that quality, even though others might laugh at us for honoring our own special unique qualities. It is especially difficult when others make fun of us at a young age, although, that ridicule only makes us stronger. Stand out, be confidently different, celebrate life because that uniqueness will make you happy and you will be discovered eventually. Just enjoy this time in your life. The younger you accept this about yourself, the better, as it will save you a lot of heartache about not fitting in. The less you fit in, the more special and talented you are. I know this is a hard thing to be different and happy about being different. We usually want to blend in and be loved. In the end, you will only love yourself and be lovable to others if you separate yourself from them. The earlier you do this, the better, as you will give yourself more time in life to attain a higher degree for your talents to blossom. Be your own star, until others see your star shine through. You need a certain amount of time alone to think about who you truly are and to think about your own special uniqueness. This is how you can dream more. Remember, daydreaming is your creative thinking time. Don't be misled by others trying to mislead you from your own special uniqueness. Anytime you say to yourself that you have not been true to yourself is a sign that you should not go down the path others have tried to set for you. Just Remember, you are your own true path. Set a shining path for others to follow.

Do not go where the path may lead,
go where there is no path and leave a trail.

RALPH WALDO EMERSON

Express Your Pathway
Marcy on The Orient Express

Chapter 5

THINK IN LAYERS

Your enjoyment in life is directly related to how you think. Asking the next question is always crucial, otherwise you have shallow thinking. The next question will take you deeper into how things got to be the way they are, and of course, makes you more interesting to yourself. Being more interesting to yourself will make you more interesting to others. Why is this important? Life is in the details. You can only notice the details if you think deeper. Little details add interest and make for a big life. A big life can be lead whether you are rich or poor. When you are poor, creativity is your best friend and will add zest to your life. If you are rich, creativity is still a must. The materials at your fingertips are so much greater, although wise choices still must be made, as no one has unlimited funds, ever. Quality is always a necessity, otherwise you wind up with quantities of no importance and even a junked up life.

Don't ask what the world needs. Ask what makes you come alive and go do it, because what the world needs is people who have come alive.

HOWARD THURMAN

Chapter 6

ALTARS

❧

You need altars for your creations. By that I mean you need several counters, table tops, coffee table tops, desks tops or any tops that are just that, your designated sacred altars to express yourself. They need to be yours and yours alone, not for objects placed there and never changed. This is your ever revolving canvas. Decorate these altars according to season or entertaining or just for the fun of it. Use all kinds of objects, flowers and travel finds to express yourself. Start collections in your travels and use these collections on your tablescapes. This is a small joy in your life, but this is one place that you can have all to yourself for creating the landscapes that live in your mind. They are in there and you will be surprised at the ideas and creativity this can produce within yourself. Certainly use old objects around the house, anything and everything is fair game, a dress for a tablecloth, a glass turned upside down for a candleholder, a skirt under a centerpiece, and bracelets as napkin ring holders. In other words, use the MacGyver in you. This makes your mind do agile tricks with objects you have and can be done quickly, inexpensively, on a small scale, for a big result. Don't be too matchy, this is someone else's idea of what you should do, matchy is not for you. Have fun.

Creativity is not the finding of the thing,
but the making something out of it after it is found.

JAMES RUSSELL LOWELL

222

Chapter 7

SIMPLICITY

Simplicity is overrated. Don't be too simple for your own good. Simple is not interesting in itself. It is only interesting in relationship to anything placed in juxtaposition to it. A beautiful woman in a simple black dress, for instance, is different that a plain woman in a simple black dress. The plain has to accessorize, the beautiful does not.

I have often heard of couples that want to simplify their lives, sell or give away their objects and scale down. I wonder why? Why would you want to give up your history and negate all of the time you spent gathering these lifelong items? So choose wisely. There is much to say about not just getting things and cluttering up your life with these objects, just to get them. Don't spend any time on this. If you can't get what you want, make do and save for quality. If you just get things, you will have to replace anyway and that quantity will cost as much as the quality in the long run.

Simple can only be beautiful if it is quality. Quality combined with quality is beautiful, comforting and enduring. It makes us feel better and at ease with the world. If I want starkness, I will get that in my hospital room, not my living room. So, don't simplify in your life and certainly don't simplify just to simplify, know what you are doing in relationship with everything around you. Don't give up on your life; that is really being dead before you actually are. Simplifying leads to predictability and regularity and is the opposite of your creativity and reinvention. It also leads to doing the same over and over again, which only can lead to

23

dissipate you from your energy and abilities. So, I never want to hear anyone say, keep it simple or I want to scale down. Never. Simplicity is easily graspable to everyone and that is the opposite of what you are becoming, an artist. You are changing old things in new ways. Don't ever give up your history for the sake of simplicity, and don't be swayed by others, who are doing this, this is not for you. Your history is your life's work, ever changing. So why cut out the heart of your story, for what, for the sake of simple. Simple is different than the quality of understatement; don't confuse the two. You don't have to be educated to be simple, but you are probably educated if you understand understatedness. Pure and simple, that is.

More is more.

ADAM LAMBERT

Adam Lambert Concert
Mystic Lake, 2010

Chapter 8

YOU ARE ALWAYS BEING JUDGED

ॐ

You are always being judged for your looks, your dress, your manners, for the way you carry yourself, your voice, just to name a few. The eyes blink and they know. Within seconds, you are being judged for acceptance or rejection. Of course, you can change these perceptions over time but they are nevertheless how you are presenting yourself to the world. What do you want to accomplish at what time? Appropriateness is usually the best choice, but not always. How to distinguish yourself from the fray and be admired and not criticized is a fine line and one you have to choose at all times. Blending in is overrated and boring. Why bore yourself when you don't really want to and why bore others? Uniqueness does not make up for a lack of talent. You always have to be talented or at least always working on your talent. In some ways, working on your talent is more interesting than having talent. You will eventually be rewarded for your talents. Always be yourself. Don't let others define you, put you down or tone you down. You can be reassured that others will see and want you to be less of yourself, that only endures you to them and gives them power over you. Your power is in creating and recreating your snowflake, the one and only you. Only you can put the energy of the detail of what you notice and create into who you truly are. So you are always reinventing and changing who you are and only you can keep up with yourself. Others don't have time to keep up with you. Remember, they don't care about you as much as you care about yourself. I keep repeating this, but this is important to remember because others can only pigeon hole you in time and space and most are only in your life for spurts of time and can't see the ever changing you. A stronger and newer you is emerging and can be intimidating to those who want to put you in a place where they can keep you forever stagnant. Squirm out and don't let them do to you or speak for you. You are your own best presenter and speaker. Just Remember, speak out and be judged for who you are and not what others want you to be.

I don't know the key to success,
but the key to failure is trying to please everybody.

BILL COSBY

A Bird Being Judged by its Feathers
Hawaii

Chapter 9

CREATE GOALS

E very few years or so, write down, yes, write down what you want to achieve in your life in these specific areas: physical or sports goals; education goals; travel goals; family goals; job related goals; artistic and hobby goals. If you write down your goals in these areas and regularly review them, you will accomplish these goals, or they become a nagging part of your memory until accomplished. It has been demonstrated time and time again, if you write down what you want, your chance of success becomes likely. Even in Weight Watchers, if you write down what you eat every day, you lose weight and if you don't, you don't lose weight.

Of course, you are the navigator and the captain and the crew of your ship. So only you can set a course, follow it, chart it, correct it and do all of the work. Remember, others don't care about you as much as you care about yourself. So beware of the naysayer, the advice giver, the flatterer, the interferer and the crew, when you are accomplished enough to have one. Only you are in charge of your own ship. Never forget that. Listen to others, but make your own decisions and be aware of what is best for you in your life, right now. Only you know for sure the destination of your journey. And always, always, have a plan. In life, some people are finders, some binders, some grinders and some minders. At first, you have to be all of these things. The highest level is in the end to wind up as the finder or at least the binder, never the grinder or the minder. That is unless you love the small details and are not happy being on top.

It is important, once you have established what your goals are, to start and to finish. Some people are great starters, others are great at finishing. You must be both of these, even if you are slow to start; you must be steely to the finish. Don't let anything or anyone distract you. Until you have achieved the status of the finder, you must do all to the finish. So, Just Remember, accomplished goals start as written goals.

You can't build a reputation on what you are going to do.

HENRY FORD

Small Goals Create a Larger Picture

Chapter 10
FACE YOUR FEARS

The thing that you fear the most is the thing you most need to do. Always attack your biggest fear and you will become stronger as a person and not be a weak victim to your fears. Others will see your fears more clearly than you do, some will try to help you with yours fears and others will try to hurt you with your fears and still others will want to play into your fears to identify with them more. You alone know that you are a work in progress. Keep attacking your biggest fears, but also know that when you overcome your biggest fear, that other new fears will crop up to try to beat you down and make you weak again. You will know what this next biggest fear is when you dread facing it. Although, don't ever think that you have to face a dangerous fear, such as scuba diving or sky diving. Always, keep in mind, that you will not be able to overcome your fears right away. Practice doesn't always make perfect immediately. Keep in mind, your new found lack of intimidation will give you new found powers and you need these powers to be in control of your life. Keep trying, and don't ever be afraid to look dumb or stupid or incompetent in the beginning. You might even surprise yourself and find you are quite good for a beginner. If you want something bad enough, you will need to have small goals to eventually achieve a big result. Realize there is no such thing as perfect. You must strive for the best version of perfect imperfection that you can, but strive you must. Just Remember, go towards what at first feels unnatural and you will become a natural.

Marcy Kruchten

Fear makes the wolf bigger than he is.

GERMAN PROVERB

You are limited only by your fears.

FRAN WATSON

Olivia
Riding Lessons with Chewey 2006

Chapter 11

LIVE IN THE PRESENT

ᕫ

Live in the present, not the past, not the future. If it is here and now, don't dismiss it, live it, do it. Take advantage of it. Don't think that when something happens in the future, it will make you happy. Even if it does happen the way you thought it would, it doesn't guarantee happiness. Happiness is always in the present. Remember, the past is 20/20 hindsight, because if we had known better, we would have done differently, and there are things we might not have done at all. Regrets about the past are only okay if we can change them somehow in the present. Past regrets should be learned from and not dragged on and on to interfere with living today. Change your life dramatically if you regret anything in it.

I was standing at the Glockenspiel in Munich and every thirty seconds a bell rang signifying how quickly life passes. Do something. Don't waste time unless you are thinking, resting, daydreaming or sleeping. Remind yourself often to do it now, when the opportunity is here. It soon passes and circumstances change so rapidly that we must act now and make decisions quickly sometimes. Just make a decision, "just do it", as Nike says. Any decision not made, is in itself a decision, so make your decision, or one will be made for you. Make rules for yourself and keep them close to you, live by them and remind yourself about these principles of life frequently. Just Remember, don't let the past rob you of a future to live in the present.

*The best thing about the future is that
it comes one day at a time.*

ABRAHAM LINCOLN

Marcy, Georgia, Lisa, Olivia
Easter 2006

Chapter 12

BE A STUDENT

Know that you are always a student all of your life. You can learn from everyone and I mean everyone. Everyone has something to teach you. Always be interested, if only for humor's sake, if nothing else. Try to amuse yourself, but learn from your inattention that you have missed an opportunity to learn something. Why? Because we have surroundings around ourselves and they are only interesting if we know more about what they are. This will make for a more interesting life and in the very least keep your mind agile and prevent mental deterioration. Try new fads, new foods, new things, new ideas on every level that you can. Don't ever say you don't eat fish, for instance (of course, unless you are allergic to shellfish) or make up stupid excuses for yourself that puts you in little boxes and corners you from what the world has to offer. Just Remember, you are young only once and might not always have the opportunity if you pass up a once in a lifetime opportunity NOW. You are here, now; trying it can only add to your life experience. Why subtract and cut yourself off to spite your face? Why? The only time you should choose nothing is when you can only have something not worth choosing. But of course, you will only know what is worth choosing if you try everything you can. Always go for the best and choose nothing rather than mediocrity. Just Remember, if you haven't learned and tried to learn more about what is the best, you will choose and be mediocre yourself. Set your standards higher and change your mind to even higher standards. Always, choose quality above quantity; that goes without saying for you. Have only one geranium plant that you tend to until it is beautiful, rather than fifty plants that you cannot take care of and let die. Quality does count and you will attract other quality individuals as quality attracts quality. Mediocrity attracts mediocrity. Aim for the highest happiness in this way.

The unexamined life is not worth living.

SOCRATES

Enjoying a Minnesota Snowfall 2006

Chapter 13

ASK AT LEAST THREE QUESTIONS

When you first meet someone, always ask them at least three questions about themselves. It is only polite. It shows interest. You will learn a great deal about what interests, motivates and disturbs people from all age groups and all parts of the world. You already know what you think about a topic (so you don't have to bother asking yourself). The question is, what do they think? That information can be useful information at a later date, whether it is just amusing, useful information, anecdotal or just downright funny. We can always learn from everyone, whatever the topic. These questions make you more interesting to number one, yourself, and then to other people. But, one condition; don't feign interest in others. They will be able to tell if you are just asking inane questions and have no interest in the answer. This is insulting to them and their intelligence and using them as prey. No one likes being used as prey. They will be able to tell if you are just asking them a question to be used against them at a later date. Remember you are not a psychiatrist analyzing a patient on the couch. People know this and can sense it. If you become the grand inquisitor, this technique will make you less connected, rather than more connected to people. Always ask two to three questions and then shut up. And for God's sake, don't interrupt after one question with your own answer to your own question. Use where, what, when and why. Why is always used later, as why can be construed as prying if used too soon. Remember, you are using questions to sit a little closer to someone you instinctively like and want to get to know a little better. Always sit a little closer, but don't commit too soon. Decide on your interest, if you want to get closer. But in any case, questions are a way to learn more about anyone. Without questions, we are our own worst monologue going on and on about ourselves. Keep them going with questions and you will learn more than you ever planned. Just Remember, you already know what your answer is to the question. What is theirs? Everyone is your teacher.

You can't fake listening. It shows.

RAQUEL WELCH

Asking Three Questions
Cuzco, Peru

Chapter 14

ASKING QUESTIONS
(GLEANING INFORMATION)

This is a little different than asking questions to draw someone out or to get closer to someone you might have an interest in. This is about getting the answer to information that you genuinely want to know.

Don't be afraid to ask that question that you don't already know the answer to. Just Remember, that question lets others know how far you have come and what your education is. Keep in mind that you can give others power over you as they realize that you are neither as well educated or as well traveled as they are. You still have to ask because if you don't, someone else will. You will realize that your question is the question that gets to the heart of the matter, and makes everyone think about the right answer. So ask that thoughtful kind of question, not the naïve one that negates your power. Just Remember, don't ever be that person that asks a question that is a monologue so long and under such pretense that you are some kind of an Einstein, when in fact you are asking a question to Einstein.

Judge a man by his questions rather than by his answers.

VOLTAIRE

Chapter 15

PROCRASTINATION

Procrastination is only good in the dreaming, thinking and planning stages. Once the thinking, planning and dreaming is done, procrastination becomes non action if it lasts too long. How much time is too long a time? When you sit and think about something over and over again, that is when it becomes procrastination. Going in circles is one of your biggest enemies. It delays self actualization. Just make sure you have gathered the facts and that they are accurate before you begin but don't let perfection delay you. Sometimes after an idea is implemented, it engenders new ideas and takes on a different form. You won't know what form your style will take until after you have begun. Just Remember, there is no such thing, ever, as perfection and the imperfect is always your most perfect and yours alone. So begin.

Remember, don't pay too much attention to anyone else's style or you will become a blend of their style and your own style. Blind yourself to others style and you will become more of yourself, rather than more of them. When I was a greeting card designer, I went to the yearly New York Stationery Show. I purposely did not go around and look at other greeting cards because I might be too influenced by their ideas and not come up with my own. This served me well over the years, as I did observe that many artists complained that this blending of styles happened to them. A blending of styles will never be considered to be one of the great designers. These are copiers and at their worst, copyright infringers. Don't fall into this trap, be a true original. Once you have started, wear blinders.

That is not to say you are not always paying attention to new ideas and trends, but don't be too influenced by one trend or one artist.

Inaction breeds doubt and fear. Action breeds confidence and courage. If you want to conquer fear, do not sit at home and think about it. Go out and get busy.

DALE CARNEGIE

Orient Express Venice to London 2005

Chapter 16

PATIENCE AND PERSEVERANCE

ॐ

You need both patience and perseverance in your life, but perseverance is the key. Patience is a matter of time but without perseverance, is dead time. It is never a matter of just waiting; action is always required through perseverance. Hard decisions require a certain amount of suffering and often patience and thought, but, ultimately always require action. After choosing your dream, it may not come through to the highest level at first, just persevere with patience, but especially choose more action. Be careful when you choose a dream to follow, make sure that it matches closely with your natural talent, so you will need less time, through patience and perseverance, for it to come true. What is the main difference between patience and perseverance? Perseverance does not mean blindly following the same path but rather adjusting as necessary, doing what is necessary and not giving up when others often do. Just Remember, perseverance is often the main differential quality between those who ultimately succeed and the also-rans.

Patience is bitter, but its fruit is sweet.

MAHATMA GANDHI

Chapter 17

A SENSE OF HUMOR

❧

Humor should be called the sixth sense. Just like we live to see, hear, taste, touch and smell, we live to laugh. We act crazy to remain sane, we laugh to live a sane life.

Laughter is getting and a sense of humor is giving.

What do we laugh at? What makes something funny? What is a sense of humor?

What one person finds funny, another person might find insulting. Sarcasm is only funny if we make fun of our own weaknesses, not the weaknesses of others, at least to their faces. (Now that was supposed to be funny hah!). What surprises us in a very pleasant way often makes us laugh. Contrast can be very funny, as it is the juxtaposition of opposites that come at us from different angles. So expecting one thing and getting the unexpected can be fun. The key here is in the fun of letting go on the control of life.

Laughter is our connection with love. Why else do we always describe what we look for in a potential mate as, "they must have a sense of humor."

I have found over the years that I don't enjoy canned jokes, however well told, nearly as much as little tidbits or stories about life's little foibles.

Remember, your sense of humor shows your class, your prejudices, your political leanings, your taste and your sense and sensibilities on life. So be kind and not too sarcastic.

Just Remember, laugh at yourself and with others.

To appreciate nonsense requires a serious interest in life.

GELETT BURGESS

Thinking In Layers
Venice, Italy 2004

Chapter 18

BEING A LEADER

❧

A leader is different than being a boss. A boss may rise to his position without being a true leader. A boss may fall from grace and still remain a boss but a leader who falls from grace is no longer a leader. What constitutes a leader? Because you will be very creative, you will blaze a trail that will lead people to you. If your shining path is wide enough, others will follow you naturally. Let others follow you, just don't let them mistake that they can become you. Imitation is the highest form of flattery, if taken too far, can become a dangerous game. Creativity is always at the heart of true leadership. You will never be the tail, you are the dog wagging. That is why others seek you out. You have lit a shining path for all to see and they will be compelled to follow you down that path. They are counting on you to do the right thing, so lead, don't mislead. As a leader, you will help others to make less painful decisions and short circuit wrong headed decisions. Just Remember, to be a true leader, you must be grateful and a follower of your followers.

If you want to lift yourself up, lift up someone else.

DOROTHY PARKER

Chapter 19

"SHOULDS"

ह

Listen to your "shoulds." If you tell yourself, you should do this or do that, listen very carefully, as it is often a priority. Keep lists of what you should do and divide these lists into school or work, household, physical, errands, phone calls or notes to write. Divide these lists daily into priorities, urgent and important and generally know the difference in the urgency of your to do lists. They never have the same priority. The hardest thing to do should be number one on your list to bring relief and make the rest of your day lighter.

Just Remember, the hardest thing undone will keep you a prisoner and will free you when done. This goes back to the pleasure/pain concept. Whatever you choose first will be quick and the second will linger. So chose pleasure first and the pain will far outweight the pleasure in the end. So make your pain become your pleasure and double your fun. And, it goes without saying, look for the humor in any difficult situation. Once humor is there, the fun begins, no matter how dire the circumstances. Attacking a situation will put you in the driver's seat of doing, not just thinking about doing. If you are taking time justifying not doing something you should do, keep it to yourself. You should never give a long list of your shoulds to anyone; this is your list and your list only. Others will only wonder why you have time to justify, and not do.

Ambition should always serve as the handmaiden to talent.

PAT CONROY

Grand Palace
Bangkok Thailand

Chapter 20

TRUST YOUR GUT

Trust your gut feeling when you think something might be going on that others don't want you to know about. I have rarely been wrong about a gut feeling. If you feel something is wrong, it is. If you start searching for evidence, you will find it. Trust that evidence. It is a confirmation that something is wrong and here is the first proof of it. You will start searching and finding further evidence, trust that further evidence. How to use this evidence? You don't have to use this evidence right away. In some ways, it is better for just you to know right now. What does this evidence imply? Think about the implications. It is your little secret and when you share it with anyone, it is no longer a secret. Make a pact with yourself, don't do anything or say anything right now. Sometimes, something left unsaid or undone is the most powerful action at the moment. If you are tempted, always say to yourself, don't say it. You can always use it later. It is information in your quiver of arrows to always have but to use judiciously. Once it is said or written down, especially in an e-mail, it becomes real and part of your history. That is when you have to do something with the information. Unless you are prepared with an action plan, your action right now is to keep it to yourself. Just Remember, pacts with yourself are sacred and your power. So don't give power to anyone unless you are prepared to have them help you with the problem.

As soon as you trust yourself
you will know how to live.

GOETHE

Marcy with her father
1968

Chapter 21

BE PUNCTUAL

৳

Being punctual is not the real issue, consideration is. Being on time shows you care about others, not just yourself. Being on time takes away talk of being on time. If you are consistently late, others will start talking about you, and not in a flattering way. They will discuss your self-centeredness, your selfishness, your lack of consideration for others and if their relationship with you is worth the insult every time you are not on time. Don't let wasting others people's time ever be a conversation they have about you. Spend a little of your own time thinking about how you can be on time so you don't waste other peoples time waiting for you. Have rules for yourself in this regard. Ask yourself if you would be late for the Queen of England. Or conversely, how long should you let others to be blatantly late with you. I have a rule: I don't make others wait for me and I don't wait more than a half hour for others, unless they have let me know that they will be late. When we were on tour in Japan, the bus driver let us know that he would pick us up at 8am sharp, and if we were not there, he would pick us up the next day at 8am sharp. That is the way of the world, so make it a habit of always trying to be on time. We all have cell phones today, not excuses.

I've been on a calendar, but never on time.

MARILYN MONROE

Chapter 22

ALWAYS READ

ᘒ

Always be reading at least three books at a time in different genres of your choosing, but always include fiction, self help and historical with world maps as guides. Learn how to improve your life and those around you, even if you only read a cookbook, cover to cover. I find I always read a cookbook cover to cover, if I am on a diet. Read the current best sellers in fiction. If you find one very talented writer, read everything that he or she has written, as these are few and far between. The closest I can get to describing their style is fluid, liquid and simmering. Don't spend any time on trashy novels other than when you are young and need to read a few trashy authors for a little sexy stimulation. Read the classics. Why are they called classics? They are called classics because they capture human nature and universal principles through space and time.

If possible, join or form a book club so you can discuss books and their ideas as they apply to your life.

Never trail on another's reading list as you will have a feeling of always falling behind and reading their leftovers, but do take recommendations they seem to truly love and continually ask others what is the best book they have read in the last six months. Have you own reading lists at all times. Try reading books that you would not be normally interested in, you will be surprised at how much you will learn and be stimulated outside of your realm of interests. Reading will teach you to notice the details in life and make your world more exciting as you travel and recognize things you have read about.

On a side note, go to movies but don't replace reading with movies. I usually have three movies that I rent per week and I usually go to one movie per week, as I write movie reviews for several web sites. I keep a list of movies that I call my A list and my B list. I sometimes like to see a movie over again, it is always amazing how much I find I miss in a first showing. I always wonder if I miss that much in daily life.

Once you read you will be forever free.

FREDERICK DOUGLAS

Never judge a book by its movie.

JW EAGAN

Starting her Reading Life
Olivia, Granddaughter, Age 4

Chapter 23

TRAVEL

Of course, everyone wants to travel, well not everyone, but everyone I know. But even those that do travel sometimes want to really be at home when they are actually traveling. They make it a point not to try new foods, observe or learn to be open to the culture or the country they are visiting. I think, "Why don't you just stay home if you are really home in your mind anyway?" So, remember, when you travel, travel in all ways, with all of your senses heightened. See the Taj Mahal; smell the mustiness of the ancient carpets; feel the smooth clear white marble; taste new foods and spices; hear the calling of the muezzin. Observe differences in architecture. Visit the great cathedrals and museums; learn their history, triumphs and tribulations. Observe the great masterpieces in all of their splendor. Make a list of ten countries you would like to visit and then go, learn and I mean really learn. You will find throughout the world how really nice everyone is. Visit not only cultural sites but go into butcher shops, wineries, farmer markets, stores and houses, if you get the opportunity. Study and appreciate the differences. If you are not open to a different way of doing, being and thinking, you are in fact a prisoner of your own mind. So many cultures have been so sophisticated for centuries, so studying these treasures can bring real enjoyment and enrichment to your life. Travel is a real part of your education and a very important part of your education. Demian, as an only child, was able to travel since he was quite young. Because of his travels to such locations as China, Macau, Australia, New Zealand, Russia and all of the European countries, he is more tolerant, open minded, educated and more interesting to talk to because he has seen the world. His travels prompted him to study the great philosophers and philosophies of the world as an undergraduate student.

One's destination is never a place,
but a new way of seeing things.

HENRY MILLER

Visiting Machu Picchu
2006

Chapter 24

CELEBRATE

⁂

Create celebrations and you draw people to you. Celebrations create punctuation to life. Without some pomp and circumstance, life would be boring. Just Remember to create your own celebrations apart from the typical already organized celebrations by others. Don't just celebrate Christmas; celebrate the birth of your own children in newly created traditions. Traditions are your family's legacy. So make them special and memorable, otherwise, why bother. Decorate to the hilt, light the candles and set the table beforehand with flowers and your own original creations. Do these things well in advance so you can also truly enjoy the moment. If at first, you don't have much money, pick the flowers from the forest or fields, use petals to decorate the table, anything to punctuate life for you and your family and friends. This will bring joy to your heart and spread joy to others as well. Learn how to cook in a delicate way, and remember, presentation in food makes up for not being a gourmet cook. Always have things set up before your guests arrive. That will make them feel important and welcomed and that you went through so much trouble just for them. Whatever you do, do not start the process of cutting up the vegetables, baking the cookies or setting the table once guests have arrived. They are guests, if they want to cut up vegetables or cook, they will invite you to their home. Don't treat them like they are workers and not guests.

Calculation goes a long way. Inviting, planning, timing, placement, delivery, and graciousness are all a part of entertaining that you can build on year after year. This can become a contest with yourself to always do something new and fun. Everyone loves a surprise, but let the surprise be done for your guests, not to your guests. Use entertaining as a way to try new dishes to cook, new ways to decorate your table, new cuisine of different countries you have visited, anything unique and special. You don't need an occasion to celebrate, create one. You don't need to think of yourself as the belle of the ball or the best conversationalist in the world, like Lady Astor, just start having parties and you will become the belle of the ball. No matter how small at first, be the creator of your own traditions.

The more you praise and celebrate your life,
the more there is in life to celebrate.

OPRAH WINFREY

Celebrating the year 2000 at the Inn
Demian, Pat, Lisa and Marcy

Just Remember

Chapter 25

BOUNDARIES

You always need to ask yourself, what are my boundaries? This will come up constantly in your life.

Just Remember, boundaries have to do with character. What do you stand for or against? Your image of yourself will help you to set your boundaries. What are your rules, tastes, morals, character? Do our rules for ourselves apply to everyone or are they just personal and individual?

It is not enough to set boundaries for ourselves; we have to let others know what these boundaries are. They can ask to cross these boundaries, but it is up to us to let them.

What is out of bounds or in bounds? This often depends if you are on the outside looking in or on the inside looking out. You have to know the difference to show respect for another's boundaries. Only then will they have respect for yours.

To expand your new found boundaries, keep asking yourself, "Do I want to expand my boundaries in any one area of my life?

Boundaries are to protect life, not to limit pleasures.

EDWIN LOUIS COLE

Stonehenge, United Kingdom 2002

Chapter 26

FRIENDSHIP

Friendship is one of the most precious gifts that we can give to others and to ourselves. Friendship requires likeminded soul mates. A good friend often knows just how you feel and often says, "I feel the same way."

You can be your true self around your friends and they will not judge you and will still love you just the way you are.

To have a friend, you must first be a friend. Friends take time and energy. So make sure when you have a friend, give them the time they deserve. It goes without saying, to choose your friends wisely.

Everyone is there to celebrate successes, only a true friend is there to pick you up from your failures. A true friend believes you and believes in you. They will cheer you on and not be envious of your success. They will help you with the messes that you have made in your life. Different friends have different advice, so listen to your friends, but in the end make your own decisions.

Friends will come and go. Even our best friends will come and go. A true friend will always be there through time and space. You can call them anytime and anywhere in the world and it will seem as though you have just talked yesterday. An old friend knows where you are going and where you have been.

Just Remember, treasure your friends and they will treasure you.

*Your friend is the man who knows all
about you and still likes you.*

ELBERT HUBBARD

Best Friends and Sisters Marcy, Angie and Julie
2008

Chapter 27

POPULARITY

P opularity takes a lot of time and dedication to attain, and of course, comes and goes. You really have to want popularity. It is not a gift you are giving to yourself, although it seems that way at first, but a gift you are giving to others. If you are giving so much to others, you might not have enough creative time for yourself. Popularity requires spending a great deal of time with a great deal of people to achieve. Is this what you really want?

I am not saying that sometime in your life that it isn't useful, but it is overrated. Just Remember, be careful that you do not throw yourself and your talent away, for long periods of time, trying to be popular. If you find you have become shallower, that is a sign that you need to get back to your true talent, being an artist. To pursue your true talent, you have to become reacquainted with yourself again.

Popularity comes from allowing yourself to be bored
by people while pretending to enjoy it.

KAROL NEWLIN

Chapter 28

YOUR PERSONAL PRINCIPLES

ॐ

Your personal principles don't need to be religious, just righteous. Remind yourself of your principles often. Don't associate with people who are not honest, lie, cheat or steal. Never do these things yourself and never ever tell a lie and never let anyone else talk you into telling a lie for them. This will teach them the principle of not lying just by saying that you do not lie for anyone including yourself. Don't associate with anyone whose principles are far below your own. This will drag you down into always having to make decisions that really should not have to be made daily. If you start to associate with anyone and find this is the case, you need to leave this person far behind you. Trouble is bound to catch up with them and you don't want to be there when that happens. The consequences can be insignificant or they can be deadly. Some of the principles below are enlightenment that have worked over the centuries.

Here are some of the principles of integrity that I follow:
Don't lie
Don't cheat
Don't steal
Honor everyone around you as if an equal
Don't destroy nature
Treat everyone with respect
Give without regard to getting
Remember your friends

Don't burn bridges
If someone has damaged you purposefully, get revenge
Don't trust anyone to do the right thing
Keep close to your roots with a little hard physical work
Take risks
Don't make mountains out of mole hills
Don't be disloyal
Don't be lazy
Don't be too smug or snooty
Apologize when you are wrong

Character is power.

BOOKER T. WASHINGTON

Visiting Demian's Alma Mater
Notre Dame 2010

Chapter 29

KEEPING SECRETS

ϑ

Just Remember, to go far you will need to keep your secrets near. A secret is just that, a secret. When you tell anyone, or just your best friend, it is no longer your secret, it is theirs too. Even if they swear not to tell, they will tell at least two people, their best friend and their husband, as a husband is thought to be themselves. If they have a sister or a mother, they will also tell them as well, and they in turn will tell their husband, their best friend and their mother. Your secret is now your enemy, as you have given out unwanted and possibly damaging information about yourself. I ask, if you have told a friend confidential information and they use this information to damage you, are they really a friend?

If someone tells you a secret, you need to hold it to your heart. If a secret is divulged, it usually leads to a string of other deceits, lies and cover ups. It is much too messy to toy with. A friend should know what information is confidential, but sometimes it is necessary to emphasize the secretive nature so they don't innocently divulge this information. If a friend consistently divulges other confidential information to you, that will be a sign that they will divulge your confidential information to others. They are telling you who they are, believe them.

And especially, don't tell others how badly you have been mistreated. They will appear to come to your rescue, but later will use this information against you. If they know that you don't value yourself or let others treat you badly, then why should they value you? This is very subtle.

Never, ever, give out free information, that if divulged, will damage your reputation or the reputation of a loved one. Always protect your loved ones and they will honor and protect you back. That is what loyalty is all about. This army of loved ones is all you really have in this world. If things go badly or wrongly, they will protect your back. That is not to say they do not know your faults, or you theirs, but you have nothing to gain, period, by divulging these faults. Don't be unfaithful. Unfaithfulness is giving a license for others to steal from you. Just Remember, when you are giving away control of your life, others will be in control of you.

I usually get my stuff from people who promised somebody else that they would keep it a secret.

WALTER WINCHELL

To Go Far, Keep your Secrets Near
Hester Park, St. Cloud, Minnesota 1982

Chapter 30

HOW TO HANDLE ENVY

❧

If you are slim or beautiful or fantastically successful or rich or all of the above, get ready, others will envy you. Your enemies are your enemies because they have studied you and know exactly what you have and want what you have. Otherwise, they would not be your enemies. Your enemies are busy criticizing you, of course, behind your back. Some of these truly want to be you and would if they had the chance. This type can be dangerous, as they can get so involved with their envy that they drum up schemes to become you, "The Talented Mrs. Ripley's" of this world. I always call these people "the ants and the termites," as they are busy building themselves up and tearing you down. Let them do it, it stymies their growth, not yours. The more you can concentrate on your own growth, the less time you have to be unhappy about others, a point the ants and termites do not understand.

When does admiration become envy? They are twin sisters, one admirable, one evil thinking. Admiration becomes envy when you are not happy for another's success but sad or angry because you don't have what someone else has and usually feel like you are more talented or deserving. Of course, to be envious of you, usually they have to know you quite well, otherwise what would they know to be envious of. Envy can quickly turn into a dangerous game as they usually perceive themselves as smarter and start to go about getting what you have. In many cases, that means stealing. This game is usually played by those who are so close

64

to you that they become confused and think they are you. If you let them know they cannot become you, they become so envious they will try to hurt you in any way they possibly can. The only way around this, I have found, is to point out they have their own special talents and instead of trying to become you, they can become more of themselves.

Envy is the art of counting the other fellow's blessings instead of your own.

HAROLD COFFIN

At Home
1988

Chapter 31

YOUR OPINION

❧

Think about what your opinion is and give it. When we are younger, we just want to be popular, so whoever we are around, we just agree with their opinion, even if it is the opposite of our opinion. We think others won't like us if we express an opinion that is different than theirs. Believe me, they will like you better if you have your own opinion and you are not afraid to speak your mind. You will become more of a leader rather than a follower and others will like and respect you more. This expressing, however, needs to still show respect for differences of opinion, no matter how stupid we think another's opinion.

First, you need to think about what your opinions are. This requires you to think about your main philosophies of life. Where do you stand on politics and the major issues of the day. You cannot have an intelligent opinion and be respected if first you do not learn the pros and cons of an issue. So, be careful when you express an opinion. Make sure it is based on facts, figures and knowledge. Be heads up and think about what issues might come up and be one step ahead. A non-educated guess only sets you back and makes you look stupid, of course, when you are not, just uninformed. Until you truly learn this concept, remember to be like Confucius, "let others think you are stupid than to open your mouth and remove all doubt." That is the philosophy I lived by when I was young and did not feel I had a solid base of knowledge and education to express an opinion. You can be somewhat excused if you are still a student, young and everyone knows you are still learning. Just Remember, once a diamond in the rough (you) becomes polished, the depth of the facets need to be there, as well as the glitter and the shine.

Silence is foolish if we are wise,
but wise if we are foolish.

CHARLES CALEB COLTON

Malaga
Costa del Sol, Spain 1975

Chapter 32

DO GIVE UNSOLICITED ADVICE

ঽ

Sometimes in the past I have found it difficult to give unsolicited advice. It is usually unwelcome, but I have realized that it is a lifeline to the young. Someone in trouble does not want to hear about their flaws. They don't want to hear about the flaws because they don't want to change the behavior. And even if they want to change the behavior, when you mention the flaws, they only hear the part about how they have screwed up and cannot concentrate on changing.

Why is it so difficult to hear about our flaws and not the part about how much we are loved? Usually change is the most painful thing we can do and that is not easy to embrace. Love is taking the chance of giving unsolicited advice. Why else would anyone risk losing love?

Advice is what we ask for when we already know
the answer but wish we didn't.

ERICA JONG

Chapter 33

THE FLATTERER

Flattery can be power. But overdone, it is a source of amusement and a disappointment in the sincerity of the flatterer. At first, we always want to believe the flatterer, that we are the best in the whole wide world at doing or being. But the exaggeration, we realize, is false in the end. We realize the flattery has been used as a toy to gain our favor, to take from us, not to give to us. We realize and are willing to hand over power to the flatterer because of the way it makes us feel about ourselves. This is okay, sometimes, as this can be mutual friendship and at its best, love. The way others make us feel good about ourselves when we are with them is love. When we realize that the flatterer is an equal opportunity flatterer, that is, we realize that they flatter everyone around them equally, this makes us feel that we are not that special, after all. I call these people super flatterers, as they exaggerate this flattery to everyone around them only to feel special themselves. Eventually these kinds of flatterers are found out and lose their powers, but this usually takes some time as most people bask in these falsehoods. The flatterer usually wears a mask to gain closeness to some of your powers. So, Just Remember, be aware of the super flatterer and question their motives before they disarm you of your strengths. Not to say that a compliment cannot go a long way, this is a tool to be used in your toolbox, but this is different from the exaggerated manipulative super flatterer.

*He that flatters you more than you desire either has
deceived you or wishes to deceive.*

ITALIAN PROVERB

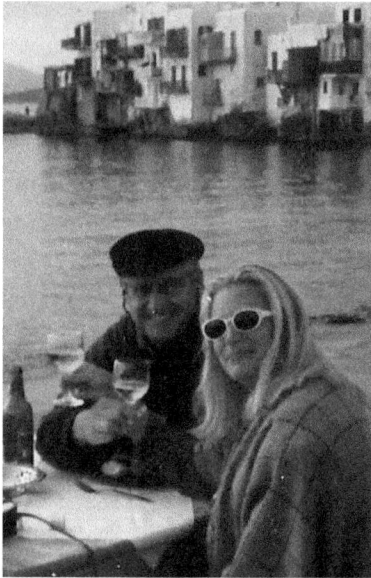

Opa!!
Mykonos, Greece

Chapter 34

GREETINGS

The big hello and the big goodbye are more about bluster than substance. But even then, sometimes, bluster goes a long way. I have noticed that the great and excited greeters and the big hello's and the big goodbyes are a lot more popular. They don't have to have great content in between. The ones with the weak hello and the weak goodbye suffer even if they have great content in between. So work on an enthusiastic hello, especially. Some will even mistakenly think you are glad to see them and care about them.

Remember their names and you will get a lot of brownie points. Even if you are terrible at remembering names, like I am, develop a "how nice it is to see you darling" technique. Enthusiasm shows confidence and that you expect yourself to be welcomed in a big way. You get back what you expect to get but you must show giving first. Isn't this true with so many things, always giving first, and the getting will take care of itself. Just Remember, if you make other people seem important, you become important in their eyes.

Love life and life will love you back.
Love people and they will love you back.

ARTHUR RUBENSTEIN

Chapter 35

MOUNTAINS OUT OF MOLEHILLS

Don't make mountains out of molehills. When you make a small problem into a large problem, you become the main problem. Making a mountain out of a molehill is a lie to yourself and a colossal waste of others time. This habit is a lie to yourself to get other people's attention. When you get others attention in this way, they will start to think of you as small minded, selfish and self absorbed. Molehills are usually a sign that you need larger problems in your life. Just remember, reach for a dream of climbing mountains, so you don't have to make molehills out of them.

Things are never so bad they can't be made worse.

HUMPHREY BOGART

Chapter 36

DON'T BE TOO TRANSPARENT

ૈ

We all want the best for ourselves. How far is too far in getting what we want all of the time? It is too far when we give up our long term self respect for petty and immediate needs. Sometimes we are just too needy. This is always the mistake trap. The danger zone is always when we are mad, sad, desperate or needy. Eating our self respect is long lasting and sometimes never recoverable. So, when you are thinking about giving up a little self respect, you might be giving up a lot more than you think. The later suffering is far more disproportionate to the small gain. So, if you make a pact with the devil, you just might wind up wearing Prada (God forbid).

In this world there are only two tragedies.
One is not getting what one wants, and the other is getting it.

OSCAR WILDE

Chapter 37

THE INTELLIGENT FOOL

Defend yourself against subtle and not so subtle stabs, deliberate snubs or cutting remarks. Know the difference between positive constructive criticism and just plain attacks on your character. Know your own weaknesses. If attacked by someone who knows these weaknesses and attacks you in these areas anyway, it is just plain mean. Your enemies only attack you in these areas, never your friends or loved ones. Get away from your enemies or defend against these attacks. Cruelty, physical or emotional pain is not acceptable to you. Develop defensive techniques in advance to ward off any attacks. One simple technique is just to ask them to stop doing the offensive behavior. Tell them they can do better than that and that you realize it was a mistake on their part and expect them to do better. Usually rising above the insult is the best technique. Showing love where there is hate is a very powerful technique. If you do not defend yourself immediately, you will be attacked over and over again and they will start practicing on you for future bigger and stronger enemies. Speak up for yourself and others so you don't become a victim or leave the situation so you don't become one. Never use violence or retort with hate as it brings you down to their level. Just Remember, don't accept these attacks, speak up for yourself and you will never become the intelligent fool.

*The heart of a fool is in his mouth,
but the mouth of a wise man is in his heart.*

BENJAMIN FRANKLIN

Marcy and Pat
Slumdog Millionaire Party 2009

Chapter 38

STAYING YOUNG AND BEING SEXY

ટ

Staying young and being sexy are all about action and energy. Energy creates the young in us and radiates from us in the form of confidence. Sexy is more about energy than young, pretty or beautiful. You can be young, pretty or beautiful but not necessarily sexy. You can be ugly. Ugly can become beautiful through action that creates energy. So if you are ugly you can still become sexy. So pretty is pretty but sexy is all about energy.

When you create your own energy by following your passion in life, you automatically become sexy to the world. It never hurts to put up a little smoke and mirrors and hint there might be a little danger smoldering underneath. Of course, it goes without saying, we're talking classy smoke and mirrors.

The good news is that we can remain sexy a lot longer than we can remain young. Just Remember, young is an age, sexy is ageless.

It takes a long time to become young.

PABLO PICASSO

Chapter 39

TAKE CARE OF YOURSELF

B y this I mean, don't be so hard on yourself. My friend always says, "look in the mirror."

Be gentle with yourself; tell yourself how wonderful you are each day. Just Remember, love yourself first and others will love you back. Energy is the circle of life. This will show on your face. Put your best face forward every day. Take care of yourself every day, not just sometimes. You are all that you have got and no one cares more about you than you should care about yourself.

So make it easier on yourself, make your rules of conduct, control and discipline. The way you talk to yourself will be the energy you put out into the world. If there are things you want or need to work on, work on those things, be responsible for the good and the bad, but don't put yourself down meanwhile.

Treat yourself with respect and others will too!

Respect your efforts; respect yourself, self respect leads to self discipline. When you have both firmly under your belt, that's real power.

CLINT EASTWOOD

Chapter 40

ATHLETICS

ৎ

You come from a long line of fabulous athletes in a variety of sports; tennis, golf, football, basketball, track and ice skating. Many were all state and champions in each of these sports. Your father and your grandfather and I have been high school, country club, city and regional champions in tennis over the years.

Always have a singular sport you can do. Pick one sport and focus on that sport; it is always the one that you are already naturally good at. You will know quickly what that sport is. Team sports are great, and a must in school, but not for a lifetime. You won't be good at any sport for a long time when you first start, don't ever let that stop you. Because you have grace and natural ability, you will get better and be one of the best if you are persistent and determined. It has been determined that to be the best in anything, that it takes a minimum of 10,000 hours. Some sports, such as tennis or dancing, take as long as ten years, but just plan on playing that long and you will be good. Take lessons right away, so you don't have to unlearn all of your bad habits later, and you will have to unlearn these bad habits later. Always be impeccable with the way you play the game and follow the rules to a T; don't ever let anyone tell you that you don't have to follow the rules. Not following the rules of a game is another word for cheating. Let them cheat, this is not for you. Just Remember, you play your mini game like you play your maxi game of life, with grace, grit, dignity and honesty. You will never be embarrassed or judged a cheat if

you simply follow the rules.
   Be gracious as a winner and the same as a loser.

Failure is unimportant.
It takes courage to make a fool of yourself.

CHARLIE CHAPLIN

Determination at Age 5
Georgia, Tennis Lessons

Chapter 41

YOUR CHECKBOOK

֎

Don't let anyone control your checkbook without scrutiny. This includes any business or personal checkbooks. Open all of your own statements and balance your own checkbooks. If you have any kind of inkling or a gut feeling that something is going on with someone stealing from you, trust your gut feeling. I have heard over and over again horror stories about the secretary or the accountant, or bookkeeper, or payroll supervisor, anyone who controls your money or accounts or finances. I was prevented from checking one account for fifteen years and it cost our family seven hundred and fifty thousand dollars. Anyone who admires you, is jealous of you and wants what you have, will sometimes lie, cheat and, yes, steal to become you. The ones that can do this are the ones who you trust the most, they are the con men and con women. You have put them, unknowingly, in charge of your finances. When you gain confidence in them and they are the closest to you, you trust them and hand over your money to them. How else would they gain access to your money? I have found that these cons have the most dead pan faces and don't tell you anything (and I mean anything about themselves or their family). Remember, they want to be you and you will find them wearing your most admired designers. Why, because they have been stealing money to afford the best designers. They become you right before your eyes and you can't even see it happening because it is too close. It's a little like not being able to see the forest because of the trees.

When you look in their eyes, you are not looking at them, they wear a mask and hide behind this mask at all times.

So, Just Remember, never, I repeat, never let anyone be totally in charge of your finances.

In baiting a mousetrap with cheese,
always leave room for the mouse.

SAKE

Shiva Sits Shiva Over Gardens
Gull Lake, Minnesota 2002

Chapter 42

KEEP GROUNDED

❦

No matter how much help you can hire, no matter how many housekeepers or maintenance men you have around you, keep grounded. By that I mean keep your fingers in things, weed your own gardens and flowers; keep your hands in dirt and you will be connected to nature. Be close to the earth, wind and fire. This is what it is to be human, when you use your senses to the fullest. When you are doing the actual job, it helps you to understand the standards you want and expect from others. Don't dust around vases and expect your housekeepers to dust under them. Just Remember, you are learning from them as well. Clean your bathrooms once in a while so you can appreciate that you don't have to do it anymore. This helps you to realize how hard others work for you and how long a good job takes. It will help them to do an even better job for you because you are grounded and they know you can appreciate and identify with their world.

What we have to learn to do, we learn by doing.

ARISTOTLE

Chapter 43

BE A SECRET SANTA

B e generous with your time and money. Instead of having your name publicized for your gifts to strangers, support your own family and those around you. We always have family members that need our care and money to help them out. I always have told those that I have helped out, that I might be in the same position some day when they can help me out. Just remember, like Sting sang, "you might be in another's shoes in another set of circumstances." Life takes unexpected twists and turns. I am not suggesting that you give only to get later, the getting is in the giving. One of the main things that we give is not only the gift but a little bit of self respect, especially if we give money and then the recipient can then give to others, that is part of the circle of life.

Real generosity is doing something nice for someone
who will never find it out.

FRANK A. CLARK

Chapter 44

BEING A HOUSE GUEST

❦

Don't stay with friends for more than two nights. The first night, you are a novelty, go out to dinner and the next night you stay in for dinner. That is it. It is too much work for anyone to be that attentive for any longer period of time and I have found that this is the extent of the attention span for you as company, not the fish will smell after three days notion. Everyone has a life they want to get on with and you as a house guest do not fit into that plan. Always, either bring a thoughtful house gift, no matter how many times you have visited or treat your hosts to dinner. If for any reason, you don't bring a gift, send a flower arrangement or at the very least a thank you note as soon as you get home. If Princess Di could write a thank you note the same night, you can too. Always show gratefulness. Make your bed before you leave to show respect, even if they tell you not to. Straighten everything in sight. If you break anything, replace it with something even better or pay for it, even if it was an accident, it is always an accident. If you are staying in a very large house or with relatives, you can stay longer, but even then, make sure you are helpful and useful to your host. There is nothing more irritating than a house guest who treats her host as a servant, and expects her host to be waiting on her hand and foot. There is eventually only one foot you will be feeling if you act this way, and that is theirs, on your backside, as you go out the door. Always offer to set the table and do the dishes. After dinner, if the hostess does not have help, help her clean up. There is nothing more ungrateful to the hostess when everyone is having liqueurs and cigars in the other room and she is left to clean up. Help with leftovers or you will eventually be left out.

House guests should be regarded as perishables;
leave them out too long and they go bad.

ERMA BOMBECK

Greeting Card Designer Marcy Kruchten
watches nature as she designs for galleries

Chapter 45

OTHER BEAUTIFUL WOMEN

❦

Warning: Don't ever let a beautiful woman live with you unless she is your mother or mother in law or daughter. It is pure trouble and can only lead to breaking up of your friendship in the end. You always have to worry, worry dissipates your attention and makes you seem jealous and small at the very least. Remember, men are always very interested in sex and you are only tempting your own fate. Don't think you can go against this notion with your friend, your sister, an office worker, maid, housekeeper or certainly a nanny. A nanny is usually young and from another country. Ever see the movie "The Sound Of Music"? You get the picture. There is nothing more attractive to your man as a young foreigner who needs help speaking English and learning her way around. This rule also applies to decorators, art dealers, painters, secretaries, and assistants, anyone who is working in your home for any length of time, even if it is during the day. I once read a survey that people become friends in their own blocks, apartment buildings and offices. Because all of these are in close proximity to one another, friendships cross all lines of class and race. Your home is close proximity. This is a warning not to be too confident that it will not happen to you. So don't act surprised, if bad things happen, if you let a woman live with you, especially one that is younger, thinner, more beautiful, more manipulative and cleverer than you are. Just Remember, she is there now and you might not be in the future.

The two women exchanged the kind of glance women use when no knife is handy.

ELLERY QUEEN

Marcy and friend Pam Royal Poinciana Golf Club
2006

Chapter 46

HEARTBREAK AND HEARTACHE

ॐ

There is a fine line between heartache and heartbreak. They both hurt. Heartbreak is immediate while heartache goes on and on.

We will have our hearts broken many times in this life. Loving someone and having them love you back equally at the same time is almost an impossibility. They are cold when you are hot, you are up when they are down, like Judy Collins sings, "me on the ground and you in mid air." One day you are looked at with love and admiration and the next day they look right through you.

Erasing all of the memories of a lost love can never be done, so we have to live with the heartache and go on. Only, use the heartache to really feel yourself. Don't make the mistake of taking medication to drown out these deep feelings. The deep pain shows us we can really love someone and it will hurt. When the medication is gone the pain will go on. So give yourself some time alone to let go of something that really never belonged to you anyway and then you can go on and eventually love someone else. In any case, trying to put back the pieces might cut you twice, you're not Humpty Dumpty. You might feel like holding on makes you stronger but in the end it makes you weaker. Give yourself some time for the hole in your heart to heal, so you don't have to keep falling into it.

So send in the clowns, for now, but they won't be laughing for long. Just Remember, to truly love someone, you have to love yourself first. Find your center, and heartbreak and heartache will fall away.

Sadness flies away on the wings of time.

JEAN DE LA FONTAINE

Count your garden by the flowers, never by the leaves falling.
Count your life with smiles and not the tears that roll.

AUTHOR UNKNOWN

Sometimes We have to View the World
Through a Veil of Tears

Chapter 47

FLOAT ABOVE YOURSELF

Sometimes life can become painful. How to deal with this pain? My technique is to float above myself. This helps me to deal with the frustration and angst that is life. Looking down on these matters makes me take myself more lightly. I can look at things in a new light and find them amusing or at the very least interesting. It is almost as if I am another person looking at myself, but through my own eyes. Only we can truly know ourselves, no one else can come close, even our most loved ones.

Observing and acknowledging your pain in this way keeps you sane, free from nervous breakdowns and unhealthy conditions that are disease.

Writing down your pain makes it somehow come out of your body and frees you. I have done this in several ways over the years. I write poetry and I have kept a journal for forty two years. Poetry is a way of twisting around ideas for a better understanding of your world and the world in general. It helps you explain yourself to yourself. Listen to these explanations, so you don't have to go over the same thoughts again and again. These writings, especially your journal, are for your eyes only unless you decide at a later date to share them. Just Remember, out of great pain comes newfound powers. You will survive to a new day in a new way.

When you're in the muck, you can only see muck.
If you somehow manage to float above it, you still see the
muck but you see it from a different perspective.
And you see other things too. That's the consolation of philosophy.

DAVID CRONENBERG

Floating above Herself
Grand Canal, Venice 2004

Chapter 48

ALWAYS MAINTAIN YOUR DIGNITY

❦

Your dignity is all you have in the end. Life will throw many twists and turns, some of your own doing or undoing. You will make mistakes and sometimes have to pay dearly for your mistakes. Just don't compound these mistakes by losing your dignity. You are and will always be measured by your actions and reactions in times of stress and duress. Resorting to tactics that satisfy your feelings of rage and revenge in the short term will cost you dearly in the end. Revenge is best served cold, as the saying goes, not in the heat of a battle. You are measured by your reaction. Everyone will forget the action and focus on your bad reaction. Don't ever let the focus be on your reaction. They win, you lose. Your dignity is all you have in the end. Might I say it again. You are the injured party. If you have a bad miscalculated reaction, they become the injured party.

One's dignity may be assaulted, vandalized and cruelly mocked,
but cannot be taken away unless it is surrendered.

MORTON KONDRAKE

Chapter 49

A FEW THINGS I HAVE LEARNED OVER THE YEARS

❧

People around the world are kind and generous.

People are proud of their children.

They want to be safe.

They are ambitious for themselves and want to be respected and admired.

People universally care more about themselves than they care about you.

You cannot control people and situations no matter how hard you try.

You cannot make up enough rules to contain all the crazy things people will dream up and do.

There are black swans swimming out there and they can disrupt the best laid plans.

It is okay to be competitive, and if anyone tells you they are not competitive, they are liars.

People will be dishonest if the opportunity to do so remains before them too long and is too easy.

Change happens, whether we do the choosing or not.

Nature is wondrous.

I have to create beauty where there is none, even if it is in my own mind.

People live for love the world over.

Just Remember, make a list of the things you have learned over the years for a better understanding of your world.

Chapter 50

REINVENT YOURSELF

ᕬ

Life is long. Change is inevitable. Even if you don't choose change, change chooses you. Everything and everyone is constantly changing, so choose change, don't have it imposed on you. There are different periods in your life, so free flow into life. Free flowing makes for new experiences. New experiences take on different forms that you cannot possibly imagine when you start out. This will bring you joy and improve your spirit as it rises to new heights. You don't even fully realize what shape your talents will become, until you try. Once you have done this, it is so much easier to look back and begin a new reinvention. You will see that these fears which rose up were really just indicators of the next round of opportunities to give you experience for the next growth spurt. New possibilities loom out there for the talent that you have and thought was small. Just Remember, you become your own building block to do more and be more of yourself.

The universe is change; our life is what our thoughts make it.

MARCUS AURELIUS

Chapter 51

MUSINGS ON A MUSE

When we usually think of a muse, we think of someone having a beautiful body, radiating an aura of freshness, almost a glowing quality that is indefinable. We think of someone who will inspire a deep feeling of passion in us to create art. A muse is like a pied piper, calling us to keep coming back for more. A muse creates a feeling of great intensity and is not a copy of anything, it is the soul, the core being released, somewhat like Michelangelo carving and releasing his slaves from the white marble.

Not all of us are so fortunate to have a muse in our life, but we can look to music and museums for inspiration. Or, better yet, we can become our own muse. In other words, you have to be amusing to yourself before you can be amusing or a muse to others. Only you can release your beauty into the world. So, let yourself rise out of your own ashes, reinventing yourself like Phoenix rising.

Just Remember, have the heart of a muse and you will become one.

The most potent muse of all is our inner child.

STEPHEN NACHMANOVITCH

Georgia and Olivia, Ages 3 and 8
Wedding on Marco Island, Florida 2008

Chapter 52

RIDING THE ROLLER COASTER

Life is a roller coaster, especially if you take risks. If you are riding the roller coaster of life, you are doing something right. After all, you are an artist and the definition of an artist is to take risks, be bold and dare to be different. Boldness is risk and takes courage. You are outstanding, so don't be afraid to stand out. Risks cannot always be calculated, and that is what makes them so exciting. You have to take chances to be great at anything. Taking risks is also its own reward because you have to learn new skills to get to the top of the roller coaster. Just remember, you can see clearly at the top, but you can also fall quickly. Be prepared for the fall, ride the roller coaster up with your hands up and down with your hands up. Remember, if you don't fall sometime, you are not risking enough to learn. We all learn from our successes and our failures to new successes.

I have often said that my life has been either like *pheasant under glass* or *peanut butter sandwiches* and I have learned that I wasn't necessarily any happier with the pheasant.

If you have big money, success or fame, you have big problems and if you have a little bit of money, you have little problems. In any case, you still have problems. It is how you deal with these problems that count.

Life is just as difficult, in my opinion, if you take risks than if you take no risks at all. I have learned over the years, that there is no such thing as security anyway. If you don't risk big, the reward will be small.

And did I say never give up?
Never give up!
So, like they say at Club Med, "Hands up baby!"

*Only those who risk going too far can possibly
find out how far they can go.*

T.S. ELIOT

Just Remember
Frame Your Eyes, Hand and Heart
They Connect You with Love to the World